A.R H

REVOLUTION

Written by Blood

AUSTIN MACAULEY PUBLISHERS™

LONDON • CAMBRIDGE • NEW YORK • SHARJAH

A CIP catalogue record for this title is available from the British Library.

ISBN 9781035835867 (Paperback)
ISBN 9781035835874 (ePub e-book)

www.austinmacauley.com

First Published 2024
Austin Macauley Publishers Ltd®
1 Canada Square
Canary Wharf
London
E14 5AA

Table Of Contents

Introduction

Humans change the truth as they want to achieve their fleeting desires, and this is the beginning of the end. The dark battle begins, and they will go to war with the truth under the illusion that the truth is their enemy. But the truth has no enemies; it is invincible. In the end, this is the only thing that will remain, as it is the one that existed before the other. It permeates everything that exists to give meaning to what is. It will never be revealed in its entirety because there will be no other existence left to watch. It is everything that is, and not everything that is not. And at this moment, I can hear your fear in your silence. Maybe this is the echo of my voice; a voice that is stronger than any other voice. But make no mistake, that is not a bad thing. What is the value of our actions when there is no fear? What does courage mean when there is nothing to fear and nothing to lose? Courage means taking action despite fear. Of course, stupidity is the same, and only wise people understand the difference between these two.

Be on the side of truth and watch how the wings of light will support you on the world's highest peaks. Fight against what is false and know that death cannot kill you anymore because the truth is eternal and you are now a part of it.

Survive before it's too late. **Get up and rise from a sleep like death before you die forever; and stay, stay, before you're gone.**

Chapter 1
What is Revolution

"Revolution" means to change from one thing to another. To explain, every phenomenon in this world can be expressed in different ways according to what we see as truth and what we want to be truth, which is the result of our basic needs. The more we reveal its true essence in explaining a phenomenon, the more we can separate the truth from what is not the truth, which results in progress towards awareness, which is seeing a more realistic face of the truth. First, we must understand what we want in this world. Everyone has a basic desire in this world that directs almost everything he/she interacts with, and most of these directions are instinctively carried out by our unconscious mind. The reason is that our unconscious mind always tries to maintain our survival, and this action is one of the most basic components of mental awareness and insight. In fact, the unconscious mind tries to ensure that our conscious mind is not locked in the prison of the brain and maintains its persistence and insight towards environmental factors. All human mental awareness is built on the foundations that originate from our basic needs, and all that we refer to as consciousness is placed on these foundations. One of these basic foundations is survival. Every living being is directly dependent on the survival of the generation before it that was able to survive and reproduce. This intellectual foundation is so important that for many people, all other foundations are built on it. In a way, it can be said that other human beings who have another basic foundation other than this one, are in danger of extinction because they can be on one of two intellectual paths between survival and the other at any moment and choose between them.

Other intellectual bases are:

1. To be
2. Reason for being
3. Pleasure
4. Honour
5. Comfort
6. Improvement
7. Need to be discovered

1) To be: The desire to survive is the most fundamental human desire. The existence of any living organism is directly related to the existence of its previous generation. You could not be born unless your parents lived long enough to give birth to you. So, nature naturally eliminated those creatures that did not want to survive or had less desire to survive, which is Darwin's natural selection. You cannot survive unless you have a strong desire to survive. In many situations, even the urge for survival is not enough; other things are also needed. Luck and ability are also important players in this game.

2) Reason for being: The reason for existence is one of the most important intellectual bases. It must be said that after survival and trying to survive, a reason to survive will come next. This foundation is so strong that, in some cases, it is placed on the same level as survival. The reason for survival is different for every person, and it is one of the principles that a person acquires over time or through interaction with the environment; interestingly, it can change, but it is not so easy to change. To change it, a moral shock with awareness of the opposite or higher position than its reason must be introduced. When the whole goal of survival is achieved, a new goal must be set, because otherwise the person will experience a sense of emptiness, and this feeling is very dangerous because it may cause oneself harm. The reason for survival is one of the most important things that a dictatorial system tries to explain to its people. That is, a dictatorial system sees the reason for the survival of people in society only in line with its goals and ideals, and there is no reason for a person to have a goal other than the ideals of the dictator, and according to the dictatorial system, they are not redundant, but enemies.

3) Pleasure: Pleasure and passion are mental desires, part of which is instinctive and part of which is environmental and learned. The fact that a person enjoys a sexual act is a natural phenomenon that natural selection has caused to preserve the survival of the species, Sexual pleasure has two factors involved in determining sexual attraction. The first one is instinctive variables, and the second one is adventitious variables. For the instinctive variables, the amount of hormones like progesterone, testosterone, etc. And for the adventitious variables like how you discover your sexuality, how you find out your gender, how you compare your sexuality with others, the society that you grow up in, etc.

Pleasure can exist in many forms, from pleasure in walking, to eating and to drug addiction. Enjoying something directly is a factor of survival in such a way that if you take it away from a person, he/she will definitely either take his/her own life or act with all his/her heart to get what he/she wants. One of the big problems that dictatorial systems have is the inability to understand this issue for their society or its extreme moral deviation, and it can be said that the distinctive characteristics of a dictatorial system are that the members of the society do not enjoy it naturally and healthily. It should be noted that enjoyment in every dimension originates from a deep mental desire for a person.

4) Honour: Honour is the result of achieving part or all of the goal of survival. The need to be proud is far more important than is commonly assumed, and a person without honour sees no reason to live. You must be saying to yourself that so many bad people have existed and exist in the world, so why don't they end their lives without honour? I must say that just as practical enjoyment is considered a negative action in the first judgment, being proud is considered a positive action. Both of these notions are completely wrong. You should know that both of these needs are neutral in nature, and the only thing that causes them to go in one direction or another is the thoughts in a society that cause them to go towards destruction or prosperity. For example, imagine a society where lying is acceptable, so liars in that society enjoy lying, and it makes them proud to lie. Be careful, because being proud is an internal feeling and external factors can intensify or reduce it. A person does not need an audience to be proud of himself/herself, but the presence of an audience can increase the pleasure.

5) Comfort: The need for comfort is one of the most important needs for intellectual organization. Without mental peace, there will be no organization in thoughts and chaos will form on the waves of thought, drowning the intellectual foundations of the mind. This chaos only went in one direction, which was to eliminate the need for comfort, and the whole reason for survival will be summed up in this need. In a dictatorial system, the peace of the society must always be sacrificed for the ideals of the dictator, and the only ones who will be hurt are the people, not the leaders and companions of the dictator.

6) Improvement: The need for improvement is a basic need, like other needs, so that there is a reason to continue living. That is, if life becomes boring, it will be exhausting and, in some cases, impossible to bear. Improvement is seen at two basic levels. The first level is a person's progress compared to other people, that is, how much progress does a person feel compared to people of the same level, taking into account the environment in which he/she is located? The second level is progress towards an ideal society, that is, a person who sees his/her ideal society as a result of the progress of society in accordance with his/her political, religious, or social attitude, always needs to see that society progressing compared to its competitors. In this case, dictators try to magnify their small progress, minimize the progress of competitors, and blame the people or competitors for their lack of progress in various areas, especially economic and technological.

7) **The need to discover oneself**: As much as a person needs to discover his/her surroundings, he/she also needs to be discovered by himself/herself and other people to show that he/she is unique and unrepeatable. A self-aware being is a being that strives to know itself. Understanding the uniqueness of a human being is one of the fundamental needs of a human being. It means that man's thoughts and beliefs, and his/her logical foundations and beliefs, are displayed on the screen of the world and play his/her role in this world. If this need is not met, his/her attitude toward the world takes on the characteristics of a soul in this world who sees others but cannot see himself/herself. **And how painful is human life when no one tries to discover him/her?**

Keep in mind that each of these bases is mixed with another under different conditions or becomes a different subset depending on those conditions. For example, for some, pleasure can be the reason for survival; for others, dignity is the reason for survival; and for still others, progress is the reason for survival; pride can cause pleasure; progress can cause pleasure. All these intellectual foundations can be mixed together in different formats.

Intellectually, a complete human being is one whose foundations are fully interconnected. As it was said, all these intellectual foundations are formed based on a person's feeling of need. Each foundation is one of the basic foundations of intellectual stability that leads to awareness, that is, thoughts are initially like waves in the middle of an ocean of information, and receiving new information is like a wind that hits this ocean, and then these thought waves, which are disjointed and chaotic, after being sifted by the foundations, become consciousness. Revolution means a major and sudden change in intellectual foundations, and the deeper this change takes place, the greater the revolution will be. If this intellectual revolution is transferred to a part of society and causes a change in people's ideals and way of looking at facts, we call it a social revolution. Societies need revolution; progress is impossible without revolution. Like rain, the revolution takes away the dirt of society and prepares the land for replanting. Without rain, the land will become a desert, and without a revolution, people and society will perish.

Chapter 2
Society and Interaction

To understand what a community is, we must first know why a community exist.

In the era of the first humans, humans lived in groups in the form of families. Every man and woman formed a family with someone for sexual pleasure and to increase the probability of their survival, so that they could increase their chances of survival by cooperating with each other. These families could defend themselves against minor risks, but for bigger risks, such as the attack of a wild animal or the attack of other families, they had weak defences, and food was usually in areas where humans competed with each other to reach it. As a result, those families began to form stronger groups known as clans in order to increase their defence and food-gathering power, and being in a larger group made group decisions more efficient than decisions made by a small family. This was because of the power of deliberation, which was created through a new invention called language, which was created unintentionally and through natural compulsion to create interaction (indeed, the father of the invention is need). Later, the tribes began to attack each other, so the need to defend themselves caused the tribes to unite with each other and build bigger tribes to increase the power of the tribe. It was usually done by marrying a woman from one tribe to a man from another tribe, and it became one of the most important reasons for the unity and trust between the people of the two tribes. Gradually, the repetition of this practice made the tribes grow bigger and bigger, and governments emerged.

So, we find that the need for security is the reason for the existence of governments, and the most important part of that is the security of life, followed by financial security, that is, people used to unite with each other to protect their lives and property and those of their acquaintances. It is precisely this need for survival and financial security that leads to the unity of people for a revolution, and the solution of dictators to prevent this unity is to convince people that these are the revolutionaries who want to harm their lives and property and that we are defending them.

So, now we can say that a community is a group of people who follow a common ideal and see the fulfilment of their needs in the realization of that ideal. Community does not require you to live in the same street, neighbourhood, city, or country. When you follow the common ideals of that community, you are a community. In every aspect in which you have a common ideal, you are considered a community, so each person is a member of the community according to the number of common ideals he/she has with other people. One member of this community could be in the deep waters of the Pacific Ocean, while another is on top of Mount Everest. But the community is dependent on time, that is, it exists only for the living, because the community has no meaning for the dead, even though they had the same ideals as you, and even if they lost their lives in this way, they still cannot be with you in a community.

I know your mental desire is that the community changes over time and those who have died are still in the same community as us; me too. I want this to be true, but there are times in life when we must choose between the two. To make an important decision, choose a bitter truth (a sad reality), or choose a sweet, comforting, and in some cases, enjoyable lie.

What is your choice?

Chapter 3
Opinion

What's the point of living when we can't make an impact on the world?

I want to answer this question with another question. What is the reason for our existence? This is one of the most fundamental questions that man has asked himself/herself, and the answer is not in words but in actions. In fact, we answer this fundamental question with our performance since the reason for our existence is to make an impact in the world.

The desire for power, fame, wealth, etc. comes from the principle that we want to be effective, and these are tools for this effect. If a person abandons this desire to make an impact, he/she will suffer from nihilism, and it is this desire to make an impact that creates dictators. They want to be effective, that is, like any other human being who wants to change the world the way they want, because this desire exists in all humans and they respond to it in different ways.

We must not forget that all of us can become dictators when we respond to this desire in the wrong way. If we take the wrong path and choose the wrong ideals, we can all repeat the history of dictators thousands and thousands of times. Due to being placed in a unique environment with unrepeatable experiences and personal characteristics, each person has intellectual characteristics that distinguish him/her from others. These characteristics of thought that are affected by his/her perspective on reality, will cause the appearance of thoughts about those realities, and those distinct thoughts are the same opinion. Pay attention to the world in which we live. Without a doubt, no person has the ability to observe all dimensions of reality. Based on the science of quantum physics (which is currently our highest level of science), we humans have realized that there is always uncertainty. By receiving information about a fact and the progress of science, we can only be effective in increasing or decreasing the probability of its existence, not in showing it definitively or the fact that anything can exist in this world and beyond. It is the greatest foundation of modern science. I will explain it to you with an example so that you have a correct understanding of what was discussed.

I want to give an example of one of the most certain things in this world to open your eyes to the truth. In mathematics, the first and most basic thing they teach you is that if you put one thing of the same kind with another thing of that kind in the same group, you have two things of the same kind in that group. For example, if you have only one apple in one hand and only one apple in the other hand, you definitely have two apples in your hands. Now imagine another world, where when two things are placed in one category, they suddenly become three and you can never have two similar things in one category, and even thinking about it will cause those two things to be in the same category and be placed in a group and become three. We can easily create a form of this world on our computer. Now imagine that the main world is a world where the sum of one plus one is three, and in that world, computers have advanced so much that they can create a world like this one with the difference from their own world, that after adding two things together, the third thing will go to the main world and has no place in our world, and we can never feel the emergence of that third thing in the layer of this world.

Well, now you can understand that nothing is certain for us, and everything is possible. Be wary of a dictatorial government's attempt to solidify its ideals, which results in the unimportant opinions of individuals. Therefore, due to the possibility of this world, each person can have an opinion that is very important according to his/her perspective, and if these opinions are similar in the majority of society, those opinions should be considered as a fact (which can be changed by changing the opinion of the majority of people). To be accepted by society, even if you are a scientist who has discovered a new thing that contradicts the truth that the society accepts, until the majority of the society accepts it, that thing is not a truth.

So, what is the solution? You can persuade society to accept your point of view by using logical arguments. One of the most obvious characteristics of a dictatorial government is that it does not care and, in some cases, punishes people who hold opposing views. These punishments can be done in different ways, such as by mocking them and their opinions, devaluing and calling their opinions false, sending them to prison, torturing them, executing them, etc. A dictatorial government will punish them to the same degree depending on the extent to which they question the foundation of their dictatorship because they are attempting to scare the rest of society into not supporting them. But the main issue is that the dictator's government is acting out of fear, not just any kind of fear, but the most fundamental one, which is the fear of losing survival. This behaviour is to preserve the basic intellectual base of every human being, so they show violence as much as they are afraid. Now do you understand the reason for the violence of dictators? Yes, yes, they are scared.

Chapter 4
Freedom

Freedom is the most important foundation of any society, so if it is present in the society, it will automatically solve all the problems, and if it is not, it will gradually make the whole society sick like a contagious disease. If there is no freedom, even in a small dimension, there will be more inequalities.

If you look carefully at the history of dictatorships, you will see that, at first, they seem very healthy and pursue human goals, but gradually they limit freedom for their opponents, and this is the first and last step of becoming a dictatorship. People in society initially believe that tolerating minor inequalities is not a problem and that can be ignored, but this ignoring is equivalent to ignoring the infectious disease of a sick person with a contagious disease in society. If you think that I have nothing to do with anyone, then don't worry! Dictators will come to your door and ask you to give them some of your freedom. They will gradually rob you of your freedom, turning you into slaves for their evil purposes. This issue will go so far in the dictatorial system, that if they could build a room in your mind to control the entry and exit of your thoughts so that it does not conflict with their ideals, they will definitely do this. And if there is freedom, it will reveal all the diseases of society and cure them.

So, what is it about freedom that makes it so important? Freedom means that a person can do whatever he/she wants unless that work harms a person in the present or the future. What harm is very important in understanding freedom? Harm occurs when a member of society loses one or both his/her life and property. Any other damage that dictators create for themselves is just a lie to justify their arbitrary actions in violating people's freedom. Freedom is so brief and pleasant that anyone, regardless of colour, race, ethnicity, religion, or other characteristics, can do whatever he/she wants without harming others. All the wealth and power in the world have no value if they are not accompanied by freedom. Wealth and power are valuable only because they grant freedom of action. What greater joy exists than being free? Being free does not necessarily bring happiness and is only a means to being happy. Being free is one part of society, and lack of freedom is one of the most important factors of destruction in society. If there are class layers in the society who are free, the society will automatically be destroyed, and it is only a matter of time. When one part of a society is freer than the other, the disease of sadism will be found in the freer part and the disease of masochism in the deprived part to the extent of the difference. The greater the difference, the freer part will abuse the other part more, and the part deprived of freedom will start to abuse themselves due to the suppression of their natural tendencies. In general, the desire of people with sadism to be in the dictatorship sector is more because the dictatorship allows them to satisfy themselves with sadistic pleasures, and the dictator will use them as slaves for their goals.

When freedom rules in all its meaning in society, it will reveal all the wounds of that society and heal them. For example, if there is freedom of expression in a government, which is one of the basic components of freedom, social media will expose all the lies and crimes of dictators, which is equivalent to overthrowing dictators, so the biggest enemy of dictators becomes the truth, and they will fight against the truth with all their might. But who will win? Will the truth fail?

History will repeat itself until the truth is revealed.

Chapter 5
Justice

Justice is one of the important concepts that I think is not understood as well as it should be. Comprehensively, justice is referred to as the equality of each person with another person beyond ethnicity, religion, nationality, etc. in social rights. But I received the purest concept of justice, not from the school of philosophy, nor from the school of religion, etc., but from physics.

Isaac Newton, the famous English physicist, obtained three laws for the way bodies move, using mathematics and calculations to predict the movements of objects and explain how to do it. These laws sparked a scientific revolution at the time. The last law that is important to us is known as the law of action and reaction. In this law, it is explained that every action of object one on object two has a reaction of the same amount from object two to object one. In my opinion, a more perfect explanation of justice cannot be found.

Now, if we assume that the condition is equal to the implementation of this law in the social aspect, that is, if a person causes harm to another person or some people, society and the law must act to return the same amount of harm to that person, and vice versa. If a person causes good to the person or some people, society and the law must act to return the same harm to that person. A good amount will return to that person. It means that if you do a bad thing, you will see the same amount of bad, and if you do a good thing, you will see the same amount of good. Pay attention to the fact that doing a bad act makes the person think before doing it, 'I will hurt myself to the same extent', and before doing good, he/she thinks, 'I will benefit myself to the same extent'. So, doing bad is punished and doing good is encouraged, which causes the spread of good and the reduction of bad in society, which is what justice wants to achieve.

Just imagine for a moment, that there is a noose around your neck and they want to execute you. What do you want? What is on your backlog that you should have done? This is the thinking that can bring a revolution to victory. The most possible damage to the dictatorship is not our duty but the only way. It is much harder to live in the darkness of oppression than to die on the lighting path of freedom. Be aware that there is a big difference between those who die fighting evil and those who want to die from it, in order to be saved from suffering.

And death laughs when it sees the stubbornness of man to live in suffering for a little longer.

$$F_{AB} = F_{BA}$$

Chapter 6
Social Rights

Social rights are the services that the government should provide to society in order to provide them with freedom and justice. Social rights are the most valuable thing that a person receives from his/her government. Social rights are the same for everyone, which means that everyone, regardless of job status (whether president or worker), religion, sect, race, ethnicity, social group etc., must be protected by the government in some way in society so that justice and freedom can be realized for him/her. It means that a person should do what he/she wants in line with his/her freedom, and the government should give a reciprocal response to it in order to implement justice. The more the response of the government is in line with justice, the better the government is. However, you can never have a government that is perfect, because in my opinion, being completely just is like reaching infinity in mathematics. Although you can never be infinite, you can approach it. Just as the number two is closer to positive infinity than the number one, one government can be more just than another.

According to the social rights of each person, in line with freedom, that is, without harming another person, he/she can do whatever he/she wants, and the government prepares the ground for it. When a person is harmed, the government must intervene and execute justice. And anyone who helps others (in any way) should be rewarded by the government in order to encourage people to do good. The duty of a person in a society is only to inform the government, and the administration of justice must be realized by the government, because the administration of justice by individuals directly causes other conflicts, but the government acts as an intermediary to implement justice.

But what should be done when the government itself is the cause of harming the people? That government is a dictatorial government, and it no longer has the authority to administer justice because it violates it and becomes a criminal under a dictatorial government. Therefore, the duty of people in society is to become the executors of justice and to implement justice, and only with the implementation of justice by the people will that dictatorial government be destroyed.

People who have been harmed by the dictatorship in society have a duty to do justice, and others have a duty to create the conditions for doing justice. Even the harm that people do to each other is the first culprit in a government, because when a group accepts responsibility for the administration of the society, it means that they have accepted that they can solve all of the society's problems. If a meteor hits the region under the government and the people get hurt, it is still the government's fault, because it should have foreseen this problem and solved it so that the people are not harmed.

Chapter 7
Union

Meaning is the most valuable thing that a human being can get in this world.

Without meaning, life is meaningless and worthless. When some people are on the same path in search of a common meaning, understanding that it is the same path can lead to cooperation to go to that common path, which is called unity. In fact, the existence of any society is the result of one or more alliances. The important goal of each person in a union is the survival of himself/herself and his/her family and the security of their property. The meaning of "property" here is not only money, but all the dimensions that can lead to the comfort and well-being of a person and the person who owns it.

Unity is one of the important principles of a society. In a society where people do not have a correct understanding of being on the same path, it will disintegrate. Without unity, society fails before it goes to battle; a society that has unity in the full sense is victorious before entering the battlefield.

Dictators usually make their ideals the goal of unity for their government, and because these evil ideals are in conflict with people's lives and property security, sooner or later they will fail. It is this unity that is the greatest strength of a social movement for the realization of the revolution. When the members of the society understand that being a dictator is equal to their destruction and that it is only a matter of time, this unity in survival becomes the strongest possible and leads to revolution.

What is more important than people finding out that they are on the same path together?

Chapter 8
Individual Revolution

Individual revolution is actually people's societal awareness. Individual revolution begins when a person realizes that the most valuable thing to a society is not its oil and gas resources, mines, or mountains of gold, but its people.

Dictators indirectly and psychologically suppress their people by instilling the belief that you are not valuable and that there have been, are, and will be many like you. But it is not like this! Every person in the world is unique and unrepeatable, at least on our planet, because every person is born with different characteristics and is placed in a different environment with other people, which leads to people becoming valuable in their specialness. People will become worthless when they do things to make themselves worthless, such as harming other people, which is a violation of justice and freedom in society. A personal revolution will occur when a person realizes a truth that will lead to a change in the reason for that person's existence.

Unfortunately, there is always a barrier between what is true and what we want to be true. Only when you understand what you want to be true can you see the truth as it is. People experience this awareness in various ways. Seeing a person suffer under a dictatorship is enough to fight against it. Another person awakens to seek justice and fight oppression as a result of the harm done to those around him/her. Another may choose to seek justice after losing a loved one. The most important problem for people who do not fight against dictators is not that they are not aware of oppression, or that they are afraid of losing their lives, or their loved ones in this way; their problem is that they are afraid of being alone in this way. Here, you should reach the realization that each person is responsible for his/her or her own actions, because when others see that you have stood up to fight oppression, others who were waiting for a companion to fight oppression will also come to your aid and follow your example. You have common pains with them, and your main enemy is known, and that is dictatorship.

Dictators are more fragile than you think because they have no place in your hearts. Dictators wield power through your silence and fear. Break your silence and start fighting by accepting the existence of fear; courage is nothing but this. Courage is not being afraid. Courage means acting with an awareness of danger, and your only purpose in doing so is what separates it from stupidity.

Chapter 9
Social Revolution

Individual revolutions and a society's intellectual unity toward the truth lead to social revolution. A social revolution is a society at war with what it does not want, in order to take control of its government and establish a new government that will do what they want.

The meaning of war is to confront the government, and the intensity of that war is determined by the government, that is, if a government only engages in political war, it gives its society the permission to engage in political war with its government, and if it engages in economic war, it gives the society this permission. It allows them to go to war with their government, and if the government kills its opponents, it allows people to kill people affiliated with the government.

Pay attention to the fact that society shows a reaction towards its government in order to defend itself, and it is the government that determines the intensity of the reaction with the intensity of its action. The best people to present this reaction are the people who have been directly hit by the government, and when they react with the same intensity to the war with their government, the society will also unite in helping them, because of the members of that person's society. They see the defender as a person like themselves, which is empathy. This act causes the emergence of community unity in confronting the dictatorship (of course, there are always people who seek their personal interests in any situation). In dictatorial regimes, they suppress society psychologically by creating terror so that people in society do not react. One of the ugliest methods of dictators is to harm the families of their opponents. When a dictator reaches this degree of ugliness, there is no red line for them, so there should be no mercy for them in the execution of justice.

Chapter 10
Action and Reaction

One of the biggest questions that thinkers have had on their minds is how to understand causality. It entails comprehending why each phenomenon occurs and why it exists in general. Almost all of our knowledge has come from how we have understood this question. In all of this amazing path, both from the atomic dimensions and the huge dimensions of two phenomena, we can say that there definitely exists, or there is an antithesis that is superior to itself in a test range, or both are equal to each other (this equality). It can even be the opposite in the absence of both.

The lack of equality between two opposites generates kinetic energy which neutralizes the two opposites. When both opposites exist, potential energy is stored in proportion to their strength, and when one of them is reduced or destroyed by an external force, potential energy is released. The opposing force is converted back into kinetic energy to return to equilibrium. This cycle of confrontation between opposites that occurs due to the unsustainability of the world causes causality. That is, there is no actual action except the first action that caused the world to begin, and the rest of the actions are only chain reactions to the first action. So, when an action (which is a reaction to a chain of reactions) is done, it creates a reaction according to its intensity, but this reaction can be released depending on the conditions at the time, or as a potential in that body that the operation performed on it is stored and released in an instant.

The society, like the government, acts in the same way. When the government transmits an action to society, society reacts to it when it sees itself in opposition to the government and the government's action. Dictators should not worry that the reaction is not as powerful as their action. I promise them that the more that time passes and the more action is taken, the more the reaction force will be stored and released explosively in the name of revolution.

Chapter 11
Good and Evil

The problem of good and evil has been, is, and will continue to be one of the most fundamental human problems. Peace will not be reached until all people have a common and correct understanding of what is good and what is bad. I think that it is inherent in a person with a healthy mind to understand it, but because he/she cannot see the whole truth as it is, he/she cannot make a correct judgment. Pay attention to the fact that its perfect comprehension leads to human perfection rather than evil, because evil existence is in conflict with existence, that is, there is no reason for an evil being to exist.

From my perspective, the goodness of any action that contributes to an intellectual basis (survival, reason for survival, pleasure, honour, comfort, and progress) in a human being (especially himself/herself) without harming a person, is better than the goodness of any action that contributes to a more important basis and helps more people. On the contrary, evil is any act that causes damage to a person's intellectual base, and the more this damage is done to a more important intellectual base and to a larger number of people, the more evil that act is.

Pay attention to the fact that when a person has to decide between a bad act and a worse act and chooses the bad act as the only possible way to prevent a worse act, it is not only a good act but also an obligatory duty for a human being. Two-way relationships are very rare and may never even happen in a person's life.

Unfortunately, one of the most used things in the language of dictatorship is when there is almost always an option to do a good deed, but dictators say we did this bad thing so that it wouldn't be done worse. Pay attention – when doing justice, that action is only a reaction to a previous action, so there is no evil in it, but as a good action and necessary to build an ideal society, it is a basic need. Dictators justify harming people in the pursuit of justice when they themselves are the main cause of everything.

As you have seen, the problem of good and evil is entangled with freedom and justice, that is, understanding them can be considered a necessary triangle to build an ideal society, where the imperfection of one means the imperfection of the other. All of this was for actions that were intentional. In the case of unintentional actions, they are neither good nor bad, just like neutral actions that neither harm nor help anyone, but you should know that if an unintentional action, if caution is not taken into account to avoid harming people, leads to a bad act, it will be considered an act that is done intentionally. On the contrary, if the ground is provided for doing a good act, then the grounding, if it leads to a good act, is like an intentional act of doing good and is considered good.

Chapter 12
Radical

Radicals in society are people who are at one end of the ideal, that is, they see the reason for their survival in the survival of their ideal. This social phenomenon is caused by the fact that they have performed actions, or that society has performed actions on them, which, in the case of a violation of the radical ideal, will call into question all of their beliefs and actions, resulting in the collapse of their minds.

Radicals have the most important effects on society. They are the most powerful weapon in society that dictators try to make for themselves based on their ideals, but there is a problem: radicalism does not have only one side and is created in conflict. That is, when a radical is strengthened based on an idea by the government or a part of society due to their radical actions in opposition to it, they naturally create a radical reaction to neutralize the action, and this opposite radical strengthening continues for so long, until the first radical is completely neutralized. The second rogue atom that forms will eventually become stronger than the first rogue atom, and it is only a matter of time. Religious and national radicals, racists and anti-racist radicals, sexism radicals of one gender against another, religious and non-religious radicals, radicals of one religion against another, radicals of modernity and traditionalism and so on, are examples of radicals in conflict.

Pay attention – the collective tendency to oppose the radical is the only way to save society from a dictatorial government with a radical ideal. This action will be easily done when the members of the society understand that the radical group of the dictator acts only to destroy them because they see their destruction in the destruction of the ideals of the dictator, and when this collective consciousness arises, the society will automatically be in a state of revolution.

Chapter 13
Government

The government is a part of society that is responsible for managing society in order to achieve the ideal society.

An ideal society is one in which there are no problems for any of its members and in which people can use their full potential to develop their inherent abilities. It is impossible to achieve an ideal society. It is equivalent to attempting to count to infinity, however, we can measure the numbers together, for example, ten is greater than one, and we can determine whether a society is closer to an ideal society or not.

Any government whose way of achieving the ideal society is not what the majority of people want, is a dictatorship. Keep in mind that the majority of people refers to those who are currently living in society, not those who have died or were not born, because everyone is accountable for their actions. The basic features of a government are the following:

The first feature: **the pluralism of the current population.**

The second feature: **moving towards building an ideal society.**

The third feature: **defending society against harm.**

The fourth feature: **not hiding the truth from society.**

The fifth feature: **being responsible for the damage caused to society.**

The sixth feature: **establishing the triangle of freedom, justice and social rights for society.**

1) The pluralism of the current population.
Regarding this feature, which is the most important feature, it should be said that the whole reason for the existence of a government is this feature. That is, if a government is moving towards an ideal society in the best possible way (according to the capacities of that society), but the majority wants the opposite, the government must follow the order of the majority, and if it does not do this, it is a dictatorial government. It must disappear. Among the things that dictators do for their government is to punish people who do not vote for their legitimacy. There are different forms of this punishment, from execution to deprivation of social services, or, for example, they limit the voting options to what they want.

2) Moving **towards building an ideal society.**
One of the most important features of a government is to work towards building an ideal society. The path of this movement should be the path that the majority of people choose by voting on basic decisions. One of the actions of dictators is to summarize all the basic work and put it to a vote only once

every few years, because the dictators have neither time nor additional resources to spend on the way to achieving the ideal government. An ideal government possesses all six characteristics in full.

3) Defending the society against harm.

As it was said before, the reason for the emergence of larger and larger communities and their transformation into governments was to be able to maintain their security against harm. Therefore, there is no reason for a government that cannot defend the people against harm, and harm means harm to people's lives and property. The right ideals do not need any defence or care, and only dictators are there to protect their ideals. They attack the lives and property of the people in their community or other communities.

4) Not hiding the truth from society.

The truth is the biggest enemy of a dictatorial system. From the time they wake up in the morning to the time they go to sleep at night, their most important thought is how to hide the truth with better lies, but this accumulation of lies is like a storehouse of gunpowder that will finally explode and cause that revolution. In dictatorial systems, people are treated like uninformed children, and dictators present themselves as caring and knowledgeable people. For this reason, they make decisions instead of the people, and they always say that, for example, if information is incorrect, it could cause a wrong impression, and in this way, people assume themselves to be uninformed.

5) Responsibility for the damages caused to society. You should know that the government is responsible for all the damages caused to a society and is the only government that oversees it. This damage can be caused by poverty in society or a child falling off a bicycle and getting injured. All damages, at any level, are the responsibility of the government. In this case, dictators employ a variety of strategies, one of which is to attribute responsibility for the incident to foreign governments and hold them accountable. My question is, how can a government that cannot protect its people from the damage caused by other governments protect its own people? What is the reason for his/her existence? Another solution of the dictator is to make the damage seem unimportant and to normalize it. For example, they might say that the same thing happens in that other country or that these things happened in ancient history, and by doing this, they try to normalize the damage. Their other solution is to blame the people themselves. For example, they say that people are poor because people themselves steal from each other, so an informed mind asks itself, "Then what is the reason for the existence of a government that cannot defend the people?" Or are people born thieves from the beginning? So, if there is theft, it is due to the poverty of the people, which can mean their property or their cultural poverty, which is one of the duties of a government to achieve an ideal society.

6) Establishing the triangle of freedom, justice and social rights for society.
No government has a reason to exist without establishing freedom, justice, and social rights for its people. A society without freedom, justice, and social rights is a self-destructive

society and will go towards destruction, while a society that has this golden triangle will move towards an ideal society at the highest speed because, with this golden triangle, all the problems will be solved by it. It will be solved. It is like a skilled doctor who shows all the problems and works to solve them.

Chapter 14
Dictatorship

A dictatorship is a government that violates any of the six characteristics of a government. Any government that is not accepted by the majority of society does not move towards the ideal society in the majority of society's opinion, does not defend the society against harm (cannot defend), or conceals the facts from the society for which it is responsible. It is a dictatorial government that does not harm to a society and violates the triangle of freedom, justice, and social rights.

As it is known, dictatorship has different levels; the more a government violates the characteristics of an ideal government, the more dictatorial that government is. A violation of just one feature of the ideal government is enough for the government to become more dictatorial, and it produces a vicious cycle that leads to the violation of all the features of the ideal government. In your mind, you can easily replace a dictatorship with the characteristics of an ideal government to understand that all those characteristics will be violated at the height of dictatorial power. However, the violation of the golden triangle of freedom, justice, and social rights is the starting point of any dictatorship, which is the endpoint, that is, when society decides to observe the golden triangle, and the most important aspect of it is justice.

In a dictatorial government, justice will not be given to the people until the members of that society become the implementers of justice themselves. Dictators have a common feature: to build an artificial world. They will surround themselves with the black and red layers, and those layers will be busy flattering the dictator to collect more wealth and power for themselves. They create a form of the world for the dictator that he/she likes, and little by little, they and the dictator believe the lies they tell each other. They distance themselves from the truth and the truth becomes their enemy. Anyone in society who wants to tell the truth is considered a criminal as much as they feel the danger. But don't be afraid of them because all their efforts are for this. The problem is that they are scared and they want you to be scared too, because whoever is more scared in this fight will definitely lose. Give them a taste of justice. Everyone in society owes it to the dictator to cause them as much harm as the dictator has caused them.

Demanding justice from the oppressor when the oppression is clear to everyone is not acceptable in any way, and it is a kind of oppression because by doing this, you send the message that this dictatorial government is right. And what greater injustice exists than to set the wrongdoer right? Your duty is to do justice, not to demand it verbally but to do it in practice. I promise you that when you become the enforcer of justice, the rest of society will join you. It is your fear that gives the dictator power. This is what some people believe, so where is the forgiveness? Forgiveness is for when an unintentional act is done, not an intentional act, where a person does a neutral act without the intention of harming another person, which results in harm to another person. Forgiving someone who has intentionally committed a hurtful act, even if it results in that person miraculously becoming a good person (which is extremely rare), encourages other people in society to do the same because they know. There is a chance they will be forgiven, but if they are aware that a malicious act will undoubtedly result in the same amount of punishment, regardless of group, race, religion, language, etc., it's a very effective manner. It prevents the repetition of this act in the future. There are specific steps to solve any problem:

1) **Accepting the existence of the problem**
2) **Collecting information about it**
3) **Dividing the problem into parts**
4) **Providing logical ideas to solve that problem**
5) **Solving each part of the problem separately**
6) **Conclusions from the results obtained from its solution**
7) **Re-examining the processes followed to ensure the correctness of solving that problem**
8) **Finding the root of the problem to prevent it from happening again**

1) Accepting the existence of the problem: The biggest step in solving a problem is accepting its existence. Denying the existence of a problem is one of the most harmful human actions.

2) Collecting information about that problem: By collecting information, you can get a correct understanding of the dimensions and ways to solve a problem.

3) Dividing a problem: It is not easy to move a mountain at a time, but you can move it stone by stone. It will be easier to solve a problem in the same way by dividing it step by step.

4) Providing logical ideas to solve the problem: Giving logical ideas that theoretically lead to solving the problem in practice, also reduces the number of times people try and spend money to solve the problem, and less time is spent solving that problem that he/she dealt with the problem only through acquisition and practice.

5) Solving each part of the problem separately: If you start to solve the whole problem at once, you will drown yourself in a large volume of work, and as a result, you will be discouraged for not taking that method to solve the problem early. Bringing partial success in solving a problem to your attention will create in you the desire to solve the whole problem.

6) Conclusions from the results obtained from its solution: After solving a problem part by part, the partial results must be collected and presented in the form of a general conclusion, and one can go to the next stage only if that conclusion leads to the solution of the problem. Otherwise, the previous steps must be repeated.

7) Re-examining the processes followed to ensure the correctness of solving that problem: No one can see all the dimensions of the truth, and that is why science is not certain. If science was certain, scientific progress would have no meaning. Don't confine yourself to one dimension of truth, and strive to understand more of them as science advances.

8) Finding the root of the problem to prevent it from happening: It is critical to solve a problem once and for all. Solving a problem at one point and having it resurface later wastes time and resources; only solving the problem for a limited time prevents this. Short-term should be done when failure to do so will result in significant losses.

Chapter 15
Understanding Dictatorship

Understanding dictatorship is not difficult when you look at it from the outside. But when you are inside it and grow, it is hard to recognize and requires high intelligence. As a result, the dictator's supporters are always the uninformed members of society, while his/her opponents are the wise. I would like to make a guess that if you examine the two populations of supporters and opponents of the dictatorship in terms of intelligence, you will find a huge difference. It is possible to know the dictator easily by examining the characteristics of an ideal government, that is, with a survey, you will know that the dictator is violating them. But we want to examine this knowledge more deeply and reveal the layers of dictatorship. We divide the layers of government into different colours so that you can understand them better. The layers of a dictatorial government are:

1. **Black layer**
2. **Red layer**
3. **Orange layer**
4. **Grey layer**
5. **Blue layer**

6.   Green layer

7.   White layer

1) Black layer: This group is a dictatorship itself; usually the number of members of this group does not exceed ten, and the death of each of them has a heavy price for the dictatorial government. At the beginning of the formation of the dictatorial government, their number was higher, but with the passage of time, their number became less and less. The reason for this is that dictators are highly suspicious. At any moment, they think that they are in danger from their relatives; that's why they will leave them with the first reason. As we get closer to the end of the dictator's rule, even this circle will become narrower, and it will go to the point where only one or two people will remain, and this is when the dictator's work is almost finished. One of the characteristics of this circle is that they are the only ones who make basic decisions for society, and anyone else who makes an important decision on their own, even if it is for their own interests, is pushed out of the way to increase their power. Others show. It's like a forest where whoever has more power wins.

2) Red layer: This layer is a group of people who are aware of the dictatorship of the government, but their interests are secured despite the existence of this dictatorship. This group vigorously defends the dictatorial government because they see their benefit in the dictatorship's direction. But you should not be afraid of this group, because when society is close to a revolution, it is this group that will either fall and come towards the people or run away. Only a few of this group will fight to the death, not for the dictator but for their own interests. One of the characteristics of this group is that they are corrupt. They are corrupt at every level, both morally and financially.

3) Orange layer: A group of deceived and ignorant people whose ignorance the dictator has imposed on them. This group is the least valuable for the dictator, and only their instrumental use is important for him/herself. One of the prominent characteristics of this group is that the majority of them have obeyed instead of using their intellect to make decisions. Another characteristic of them is that they do not seek knowledge and are only consumers of it. These are the plagues of society.

4) Grey layer: The grey layer is the general public, who only think about their daily lives and do not care about political and social developments. This layer will not be activated until they have taken direct damage from the dictatorship. They have come to enjoy life to the fullest, unaware that the dictator will not allow them to do so. They say that the dictator has not harmed them yet, so why should they fight against it? But if they know that the greed of dictators is inexhaustible, the situation will change.

If we demonstrate compassion in action, paradise will be here.

5) Blue layer: This layer is made up of people who are aware of the dictatorship of their government and want that dictatorship to disappear but are not willing to spend money to do so. One of the distinct characteristics of this group of people is that they are very sad because, at the source, they see oppression, but they feel hopeless about eliminating it. They have preferred survival to living and have killed themselves from within. It is not the dictator who is their main enemy; they themselves are their main enemy. But this group will wake up, and their sadness will turn into anger. Anger, whose tongues of fire will burn the dictator to ashes.

6) Green layer: This group of people is aware that they want the dictatorship to disappear at any cost. This group of intelligent people is one of the greatest enemies of the dictator. One of the distinctive features of this group is that they do not buckle under pressure. They want to know more and be informed every day in order to make a positive impact on society. The purpose of their lives is to make their society better. They are the main brain of society, and society will stop moving without them.

7) White layer: This group of people either exists or is a dictatorship, and the existence of one violates the existence of the other. They see the only way as the absolute destruction of the dictator, even at the cost of their lives. The most important feature of this group is the mirror-like behaviour of the dictatorship. That is, whatever the dictator does, they do the opposite; whatever the dictator believes, they believe the opposite; and whatever the dictator wants to do, they do the opposite. The more radical the dictator becomes, the more radical they become in their own right.

The important thing about these layers is that the dictatorial government automatically moves the majority of the people towards the higher layers in opposition to it until they find themselves in front of a mass of opponents, and there is no way out but destruction.

Chapter 16
Revolution's Tools

How to destroy a dictatorial government?

Sometimes, by asking the right question, half the way to the desired result, which in this case is from the same time, is covered. Anyone who asks himself/herself this question means that he/she is ready to fight the dictatorship. Fighting a dictatorship can only be successful in one way, and that is if people show mirror behaviour. To the extent that the dictator acts as a dictator, the people should react to it in the same way, that is, it is the dictator who determines how violent the struggle should be. If the people's behaviour is less violent than the dictator's actions, it is the dictator who gets motivated to do more violence, but if the people do exactly the same amount of violence as the dictator, they reduce the dictator's violence, and this process continues until the dictatorship is destroyed. Why? Because this is justice.

As we said, justice is a reaction equal to the first action. When the protesters of the dictatorship are as violent as the dictator, it gives the government the idea that everything has a price, and this causes the dictator's supporters to fall. The most important people who can spark the revolution are the people who have been directly hurt by the dictatorship. They should be the initiators of the revolution and become the executors of justice, implementing it. Finally, I have a question for them: is it better to be alive with only pain or to die to build a better society? Note that this death is different from suicide. Those who are tired of living in a dictatorial society may turn against him/her and be killed by him/her. They think they are doing a good job, but they are not; they commit suicide alone. The only honourable and praiseworthy deaths are those of those who do justice to the dictatorship with all their might and lose their lives in this way, that is, to build a better life for future generations. I think if we want to consider the meaning of sacrifice, in my opinion, it is that a person loses his/her life with all his/her strength to make a better life for people in the future.

Chapter 17
Revolution is the Solution

For those who have been deceived by dictators into believing that dictators can be reformed, I must say that they are very wrong. Dictators are not reformable. They only show the appearance of being reformable to buy themselves time and increase their dictatorial power. They do not understand any language except the language of force and power because the reason for their survival is the same. But this language is not very loyal, and when the society realizes that the reason for all the empowerment is only fear, the wall of dictatorship will collapse. Yes, yes, it's true. They do all these things because they sense death and take their dictatorial actions just to survive a little longer. But if you leave them alone in a dark room, fear will take over their entire being. Like someone drowning in a swamp, dictators will do anything to drown a little later. The struggle with dictatorship has steps that are necessary to achieve revolution. Stages of the revolution:

1. **Awareness**
2. **Unity**
3. **Make the Dictatorship weak**
4. **Fighting with dictatorship**
5. **Cleaning**

1) Awareness: Every human being has an innate desire to know the truth, and as you know, one of the biggest enemies of the dictator is the truth, and they always try to hide the truth with layers of lies. When the people are shown evidence and the lies of the dictators are revealed, anger will arise in the people against the dictatorship in their minds, the reason for which is the feeling of being deceived by the dictator and being assumed to be fools. This awareness is only for the two layers of grey and orange people because the rest are aware of the truth. This effect of anger in the orange layer of society is much greater than that in the grey layer, and it is near the revolution that this main anger will be released. People should understand that the government is responsible for all the happenings in society and that every problem they have is due to the incompetence of the government. My question is, what is the reason for the existence of a government that is harmful to the people or cannot defend the people from harm?

2) Unity: Dictators create enemies for themselves with their dictatorial actions. When a society realizes that it has a common enemy, this common enemy will form an alliance. The alliance is created when they see the only solution in the destruction of their common enemy. When dictators are unable to unite the people, they create foreign enemies for them and scare them that if we are not present, that foreign enemy will harm you more than we will, even though they are the society's greatest enemy.

3) Make the dictatorship weak: The stronger the unity of the people, the weaker the dictator. When people come to understand that their number is much higher than the dictator's, their power will be strengthened as much as their understanding of this issue, and because this understanding is two-way, it means that the dictator's supporters will lose their power when they realize that their number is small. That's why dictators don't even tolerate peaceful protests because they are afraid of crowds.

4) Fighting with dictatorship: Fighting a dictatorship entails reacting to the dictator's actions, and the intensity of the struggle is proportional to the dictator's actions. Suppose there was a natural physical law in the world that everyone would be hurt as much as they were hurt, and everyone who helped someone would be helped to the same extent. Now my question is, does anyone hurt anyone? Or was everyone competing to do the most good? Yes, this is the magic of justice.

5) Cleaning: At this stage, every force related to the dictatorship must be removed without mercy. If it happens at this stage, it will cause the dictatorship to regain power. All groups and entities that give power to the dictator must be destroyed. The bank that creates wealth for the dictator and poverty for the people, that bank does not belong to the people; it belongs to the dictator. The police force that defends the dictator against the people is not the people's police and is the killing force of the dictator. Any kind of mercy causes harm to others. The goal is to destroy dictatorship in all its forms. The more time you give the dictator, the more you will regret it. Yesterday's revolution is better than tomorrow's revolution. The biggest people responsible for gaining dictatorial power are those who leave the revenge of the loss of their loved ones in the hands of God or unseen forces in order to relieve themselves of the burden of the responsibility they bear. The most godless of them become religious in these situations and surround themselves with the illusion that their loved ones are in heaven and are doing well in order to reduce their grief and not turn it into anger. Their most ridiculous behaviour is to go to the dictator's court and complain to the person who ordered the murder about the person who killed their loved one. This is not because they do not know that they are responsible for the murder of their loved ones; by doing this, they want to calm themselves with the illusion that they did everything they could, but unfortunately, it did not work. But in reality, they are the ones responsible for the administration of justice. What is the value of surviving endless suffering? Shame on those who cause the same harm to another person by not doing justice. But when that aggrieved group starts to do justice, the fear will cover the entire existence of the dictatorial government. They will realize that there is a reaction to every action, and justice will be done.

Chapter 18
Revolution is the Evolution

Without revolution, progress is impossible, and every government reaches a point where all the gears of the government will be locked, no matter how much freedom this government wants. The meaning of "revolution" here is the social movement that leads to a great transformation in the functioning of the government, which may even change the government. Without a revolution, the government gets stuck in vicious cycles and stays there until all the features of the ideal government are violated. Antiquatedness and an unwillingness to accept new methods due to the possible risk of implementing a new method keep governments stuck in bad cycles. The greater the resistance of a government against this transformation, the more likely it is to fall. Of course, there is always a risk, but the problem is that maybe society wants to accept the possibility of risk, but the government prevents it out of a desire to maintain its structure. Even the best governments in the world will reach this point; the main issue is time.

If we go back a little and review history, we can see these revolutionary forms of society in all governments. Revolutions whose suppression leads to the government staying in that cycle and causing huge costs for the government in the not-so-distant future create the problem that the opposite movement also causes a lot of damage to society. That is, when the government takes actions with a high probability of risk without considering the opinion of the majority of the people, as is common in dictatorial governments, and what is interesting is that the majority is almost always right and has a better understanding of the future than the government.

Chapter 19
The Great Unity

Our basic question is: what is the ultimate goal of revolutions? Well, in a superficial approach to a revolution, you can say that people are not satisfied with something and want to change it, so the question is, will they achieve something that does not need to be changed? That is, will a government with ideal characteristics emerge? My answer is both yes and no. I think that an ideal government can be created, but in time it will become corrupt again, and another revolution is needed to create it. The higher the public understanding of an ideal government, the longer its durability, and this is not because the people tolerate that government more, but because the government is also made up of the people themselves. So, when the government is made up of people who are aware of what their responsibilities are, the form of an ideal government will be maintained. The important point is that no government in the form of a country can achieve becoming an ideal society. It is impossible to form an ideal government until a person enters through a door, and we do not treat that person as a human being regardless of race, language, religion, nationality, etc. The government's oppression of people outside their government area is as ugly and disgusting as the oppression of the people they rule over. People's dealings with each other should only be regulated based on that person's actions and not on race, religion, nationality, etc. People should be equally rewarded or punished for doing the same work, and their race, religion, nationality, ethnicity, and so on should have no bearing on the individual's and society's reaction. Until the golden triangle of freedom, (justice and human rights), is the same for all human beings, man will not reach peace. I hope that this common pain will penetrate the boundaries of separation and establish the boundaries of freedom on the summit of infinity.

Chapter 20
Collapse

The probability of nothing happening in the future is zero, but there is a chance for it to happen. If you don't believe, you're probably drowning in a sea of ignorance; if you believe, the same applies. Believing is both stupid and bigoted. Whatever you believe in, you are equally stupid, because believing means not considering the possibility of something not being there or being against it, and considering that one does not have the ability to understand all aspects of the truth and that there is always a state of ambiguity.

If you do not consider a chance for another form of a phenomenon, it means that you do not understand it, not that there is no other possibility. For every phenomenon, there are infinite possible forms, only a limited number of which can fit in our minds and imaginations. But we can consider a greater chance for a phenomenon to occur, and in fact, the logical part of our brain is the part that tries to know the aspects of the truth that are most likely to exist and wants to act accordingly. It can be imagined that we are all gamblers and that life is our game board. In this game, we predict what is most likely to happen and adjust our actions to that prediction. When we cannot predict a phenomenon with a high percentage of chance, we get confused, and because the world does not wait for our confusion and does not stop its movement, this confusion leads to events that should have been predicted during this confusion. Also, because they are not foreseen, they produce more unwanted results for us and lead us to collapse. The way out of this collapse is the relative stability and predictability of society, so that we can always choose the most correct way.

Due to the violation of this cycle and the war with the truth, dictators are always on the edge of collapse and remain in power only because there is no force against them. But if only a sense of stability for the future without dictatorship is created in people's minds, they will leave. No one will win over the truth because the truth will remain and they will leave. You can't block the way to the truth; you can't ignore the truth; you can't underestimate the truth; and you can't replace the truth. Truth is eternal. The truth is – what is our most fundamental goal?

Where is here?
How is here?
What am I?
Why am I?
How am I?
Am I?
.... .

Chapter 21
Awareness

Awareness means gaining knowledge about the universe and the phenomena within it, but there is a fundamental gap between awareness and information storage. Pay attention to the fact that no human being on the planet has the ability to store information with the size and precision of a simple home computer in today's era, but the level of human awareness cannot be compared to that of a computer. In fact, awareness is part of retaining information, and that awareness is like a tool that helps us find the truth. But the most important part of it is understanding the relationship between information and the functions of that information with other information. It means finding the right related patterns among a lot of information.

Consciousness is not seeing, but rather analysing what is seen. Consciousness is not hearing, but understanding what is heard. Consciousness does not touch but rather understands what is touched. Consciousness is not memorising a book; or memorising sentences; or memorising functions. Consciousness beyond memorisation. Consciousness is understanding; consciousness is building foundations to find new questions. Consciousness is not a zero or perfect score on an exam. Consciousness is simply comprehending a word, a goal, or a pattern. This is the reason why studying does not bring intelligence, but because by studying, our range of information to understand the patterns, functions, and phenomena of this world increases more and more, it opens the background for more awareness but does not directly create it, at least not with this system. In any system where a computer can get a better score than half of the students, that system has failed.

Awareness can spread through a community like a contagious disease. The reason for large changes in society is the community's collective awareness. A community's awareness of its current and future conditions is very important. In response to this awareness, society's short and long-term behaviour will change. In the current situation, when everything is clear at the level of society, a person will make short-term decisions based on his/her social level and whether he/she is from the rich, middle, or poor class, compared to whether that class is progressing or regressing. For long-term decisions, he/she will look at all levels of society. When members of the rich and middle classes fall into the lower classes and it becomes nearly impossible to move from the lower classes to the upper classes, the society collapses and the sparks of the revolution begin, or when decisions are made based on will. Even if the desire is wrong, the population should not be taken because man prefers freedom in suffering to slavery in good conditions. When they take away your will, you have suffered from the things you didn't do; it is much more than the suffering from the things you did, even if those things had bad results, but because a person freely chose them for himself/herself, then the suffering will be bearable.

Chapter 22
After Revolution

What will happen after the revolution? Following the revolution, the population will be given tremendous power, and they will believe that they can move mountains with their will. This enormous social energy, which is due to the unity created in people, if managed in the right direction, will cause tremendous progress, but if it is diverted in the wrong direction, it will be destructive. If the new government moves towards building a dictatorship instead of an ideal government, this cycle will be repeated until a government is created that moves towards building an ideal government. The initial actions of the new government are very important. Those actions are like the foundations of a building; if they are not built correctly, you may not notice at first, but once the building is complete, it is impossible to change it except for destruction (which is the revolution). The most important issue is having the golden triangle of freedom, justice, and social rights for the people. If the government can always establish these three foundations, the foundations of the ideal government will be built gradually by reforming the government through this triangle. That is, it will automatically move towards building the foundations of an ideal government. Free and critical media will play a very important role in improving the conditions of society. If freedom is limited to these media and ordinary people do not have freedom, these free media will gradually become corrupt. After the revolution, the groups that played an essential role in the revolution will start to ask for a share in the future government. This share-seeking, if implemented in the new government structure, will bring the government back into the dictatorial cycle, but, if only in the beginning they are rewarded as much as what they have done, and this issue is over, it can pave the way for building an ideal government. The initial period after the revolution is extremely important. The society should publicly express its support for those in whom it has a high level of trust. These people must have basic characteristics. The characteristics of worthy people are:

1) They should consider themselves as people in practice and not feel any racial, ethnic, religious, etc. superiority over other people. He/she does not consider himself/herself to be the representative of God, nor does he/she consider himself/herself to be God, nor does he/she see any quality in himself/herself that makes him/her feel superior.

2) They should not seek fame, wealth, or power; instead, they should seek to benefit the majority of society to the greatest extent possible.

3) They should obey the wishes of the majority.

4) They should specify a time to move their power to the basic structure of the ideal society that is presented, which they are supposed to build during this period, specify by explaining in detail what they want to do to the society and obtain permission for any basic work through honest voting.

It is true that these people are few in society, but they exist. In my opinion, the best way is to present different methods and structures and let the people themselves choose their desired method from among all of them so that the majority's wishes are revealed. No matter how good the new government wants to be, when it cannot provide a way to destroy itself through the vote of the majority of the people and transform itself into a new government that is desired by the new majority of the people, that government will eventually become a dictatorship. The reason for this is that people's wishes will change over time, and the structure will reach a two-way decision between self-preservation and the implementation of the majority's wishes. Only one choice of self-preservation is enough to gradually move against the will of the people, and the time will come when they will be completely in front of their own people. It is only a matter of time.

And how difficult it is to observe the closed ears and eyes to the truth; they don't hear its voice, and they don't see it because they don't want to. They are obsessed with finding a lie to escape it, and it is even more difficult to watch the brains that change the truth for their own temporary comfort.
Be aware that there is no sound but the truth, and there is nothing to see except the undeniable truth, and there is no comfort in anything unless it is full of the truth.